W9-AVA-160

Language Arts 809
Speak and Write

LIFEPAC Test is located at the back of the booklet. Please remove before starting the unit.

Author:
Daniel Brawner

Editor-in-Chief:
Richard W. Wheeler, M.A.Ed.

Editor:
Helen Robertson Prewitt, M.A.Ed.

Consulting Editor:
Larry Howard, Ed.D.

Revision Editor:
Alan Christopherson, M.S.

Westover Studios Design Team:
Phillip Pettet, Creative Lead
Teresa Davis, DTP Lead
Nick Castro
Andi Graham
Jerry Wingo
Lauren Faulk

804 N. 2nd Ave. E.
Rock Rapids, IA 51246-1759

Speak and Write

Introduction

This LIFEPAC® deals with the English language, which is spoken by over 400 million people across the world. Over half of these people use English every day.

If we did not constantly obey its rules and supply its needs, the form of language might begin to crumble and our ability to communicate would begin to break down. If we look closely at the rules of grammar, we can see that our language was designed to help us think in a logical way.

In the first section of this LIFEPAC, you will study English as a "living" language. You will learn about changes occurring throughout the history of English. You will study the etymology of the English language and you will examine English in the United States. You will also learn about standardization of language.

In the second section you will learn about problems in using grammar. You will learn to recognize double negatives, dangling modifiers, shifts in person, subject-verb agreement, and shifts in mood and tense. You will learn how to avoid and how to correct these sentence errors.

In the third section you will learn how to use language effectively in organizing, writing, and presenting an oral report.

Objectives

Read these objectives. The objectives tell you what you will be able to do when you have successfully completed this LIFEPAC. When you have finished this LIFEPAC, you should be able to:

1. Describe English as a growing language.

2. Explain how some of the changes in language came about.

3. Explain etymology.

4. Identify and explain certain terms used in describing language.

5. Spell new words correctly.

6. Identify and correct sentences with double negatives.

7. Identify and correct sentences with dangling modifiers.

8. Identify and correct sentences faulty in person and number.

9. Identify and correct sentences faulty in subject and verb agreement.

10. Restate the elements of the pentad.

11. Explain the functions of an oral report.

12. Explain various elements in preparing and presenting an oral report.

Survey the LIFEPAC. Ask yourself some questions about this study and write your questions here.

1. ENGLISH IS ALIVE

Students of **linguistics** classify languages as either "living" or "dead." Latin, the language of the ancient Romans, is considered to be a dead language because it is no longer written or spoken today except by scholars. Dead languages such as *Latin*, *Sanskrit*, and *Old Norse* have not changed since their people stopped using them. These languages have no more words today than when they "died"; their grammar has not changed since then and it never will.

English, however, is a "living" language like all modern languages. In many parts of the world, English is being used every day. It continues to grow and to change as other living things do. Today, English has many more words than it did in 1611, the time the King James Version of the Bible was first published. Modern words have replaced **archaic** English forms.

| English is a living language.

SECTION OBJECTIVES

Review these objectives. When you have completed this section, you should be able to:

1. Describe English as a growing language.
2. Explain how some of the changes in language came about.
3. Explain etymology.
4. Identify and explain certain terms used in describing language.
5. Spell new words correctly.

VOCABULARY

Study these words to enhance your learning success in this section.

archaic (är kā´ ik). *adj*. Outdated, belonging to a much earlier time.

assimilate (u sim´ u lat). *verb*. To absorb or become absorbed, as with knowledge.

culture (kul´ chur). *noun*. The social patterns characteristic of a certain people.

derive (di rīv´). *verb*. To obtain or come from a source.

evangelism (i van´ ju liz um). *noun*. The zealous spreading of the Gospel, as through missionary work.

linguistics (ling gwis´ tiks). *noun*. The study of languages.

obsolete (ob su lēt). *adj*. No longer in use.

standardization (stan dur du zā´ shun). *noun*. The process of making something align with a standard or set of rules.

vulgar (vul´ gur). *adj*. Lacking sophistication; unrefined.

Note: *All vocabulary words in this LIFEPAC appear in* **boldface** *print the first time they are used. If you are not sure of the meaning when you are reading, study the definitions given.*

Pronunciation Key: hat, āge, cãre, fär; let, ēqual, tėrm; it, īce; hot, ōpen, ôrder; oil; out; cup, pu̇t, rüle; child; long; thin; /ŦH/ for then; /zh/ for measure; /u/ or /ə/ represents /a/ in about, /e/ in taken, /i/ in pencil, /o/ in lemon, and /u/ in circus.

CHANGES IN THE ENGLISH LANGUAGE

Living languages continue to change for several reasons. Primitive England was invaded repeatedly by Germanic tribes. These warlike people brought their weapons, but more importantly, they brought their culture and language. The Britons were forced to accept the invaders' language along with their own defeat, and as a result, the English language as we know it today has many similarities to German.

In A.D. 1066, the Normans conquered England and forced the English to adopt French as their language. Of course, the English did not abandon their language altogether. Although English was looked upon as a **vulgar** tongue, and although no educated person would think of writing in English, it was commonly spoken in rural areas. Not until the great English poet, Geoffrey Chaucer (1340-1400), began to write in English did people begin to take written English seriously.

The theologian John Wycliffe was so excited about establishing the English language in literature that he translated the Bible into English.

As you can see from the following selection from John 17:1–3, English today is quite different from the English of 1388:

> These thingis Jesus spak, and whanne he hadde cast up hise izen into hevene, he seide: "Fadir, the our comith; clarifie thi sone, that thi sone clifie thee; as thou has zovun to hym power on ech fleisch, that al thing that thou hast zovun to hym, he zyve to hem everlastynge liif. And this is everlastynge liif, that thei knowe thee very God aloone, and whom thou hast sent Jesu Crist."

War was not the only thing that changed languages. Trade and **evangelism** also had an effect. When merchants sailed to other lands to trade for foreign goods, they had to learn to communicate with the natives. As a result, each side **assimilated** bits of the other's language. The Christian evangelists were even more responsible for the exchange of languages. Priests were commonly on board the trading vessels, hoping to convert the natives to Christianity. Of course, to make conversions, both sides had to understand each other very well.

Thus, today, English is a fairly common language throughout the world, and our vocabulary contains thousands of foreign words. Some of the earlier words are now considered **archaic** and other words have become **obsolete**.

Complete these statements.

1.1 Before the Norman invasion, English was most heavily influenced by the _____ language.

1.2 The Normans spoke _____ .

1.3 The poet, _____ , was greatly responsible for establishing English as a written language.

1.4 Besides war, a. _____ and b. _____ helped spread English and collect new words for the language.

Match these words, using only clues from the text.

1.5 _____ archaic   a. people who spread the Gospel

1.6 _____ Normans   b. translated the Bible into English

1.7 _____ vulgar   c. outdated; belonging to an earlier time

1.8 _____ John Wycliffe   d. common

1.9 _____ evangelists   e. invaded England in 1066

               f. translated the whole Bible in 1611

Match the archaic word with the modern word that you think has the same meaning.
If you have difficulty with these words, use your dictionary.

1.10 _____ shoon   a. you

1.11 _____ gavest   b. spoke

1.12 _____ doth   c. shoes

1.13 _____ thou   d. gave

1.14 _____ spake   e. does

ETYMOLOGY OF ENGLISH WORDS

Etymology is the history of a word, tracking its development from its earliest source.
Most good dictionaries have an etymology section that can be found in brackets directly following the phonetic spelling and the abbreviation indicating the part of speech.

The following example shows an etymology:

> **di a lect** (di´ e lekt), n. 1 form of speech characteristic of a class or region and differing from the standard language in pronunciation, vocabulary, and grammatical form. See **language** for synonym study. 2 one of a group of closely related languages: *Some of the dialects descended from the Latin language are French, Italian, Spanish, and Portuguese.* 3 words and pronunciations used by certain professions, classes of people, etc. —adj. dialectal. [<Middle French *dialecte* < Latin *dialectus* < Greek *dialektos* discourse, conversation, ultimately <*dia-* between + legein speak][1]

The guide to the abbreviations found within the brackets is usually found in the front of the dictionary. In the case of the word *dialect*, the abbreviations mean that it **derives**, or comes, from the Middle French word *dialecte*, which comes from the Latin word *dialectus*, which comes from the Greek word *dialektos*, which means *conversation*.

Put an X by those words you think are new additions to our language.

If you *need* help, use you dictionary *after* you have tried.
Hint: New words have no etymology listed.

1.15 a. _____ x-ray   b. _____ mountain

c. _____ horse   d. _____ laser

e. _____ book   f. _____ supercharge

g. _____ subway   h. _____ leather

i. _____ pitcher   j. _____ nylon

Complete these activities.

1.16 Pick a page of the dictionary at random.

a. List the different languages you find in the etymologies.

_____

b. Which language seems to be the most common? _____

c. Which, the most rare? _____

1.17 Look up the etymologies of the words in the following list, In the space provided write the language or languages of the word's origin and, if possible, the word(s) from which it derives.

The first one is done for you.

frail, <u>fr. Middle English, fr. Middle French "fraile," fr. Latin "fragilis" fr. "fragere."</u>

a. jury _____

_____

b. panic _____

_____

c. chant _____

_____

d. oyster _____

_____

e. oven _____

_____

f. carousel _____

_____

g. kaleidoscope _____

_____

h. interfere _____

_____

i. chintz _____

_____

j. meadow _____

_____

1.18 OPTIONAL ACTIVITY: Try to find an *unabridged*, not condensed, dictionary (the *Oxford English Dictionary* is the best) and look up the etymology and meaning of your name. You should try to find both your first and last names. This information is also available online.

a. _____

b. _____

TEACHER CHECK _____ _____
                          initials   date

ENGLISH IN THE UNITED STATES

Perhaps you have heard an English person speak and have noticed that not only is his accent different from yours, but some of his word choices are also different. For example, an English person would refer to what we call an elevator as a *lift*, a windshield as a *wind screen*, and a subway as *the tube*. If an English-man were going to have his tonsils removed, he would probably say he was going *to hospital* instead of to *the* hospital.

By now you may be thinking that the English you speak is not just English but is "United States English." In a sense it is. You live in a culture that was made up of several different cultures. Perhaps you discovered, when you looked up the etymology of your name, that it comes from German or Italian.

Of course, this country was originally settled by the English; consequently, most of our customs and most of our language derive from that country.

However, the United States has been called the "melting pot" of the world because settlers from all over the world came to make their homes in this land, each bringing their language and traditions. Unlike the Normans, who forced the English to speak French; the English settlers did not attempt to force the other settlers to speak English. As a result, we use a great many foreign words, often without realizing they are foreign. *Minnesota* is a Native American name from the Dakota People;; *Los Angeles* is Spanish; *Phoenix* is Greek; and *New Orleans* is French.

Besides borrowing foreign words, people in the United States have made up quite a few of their own. The word *blizzard*, meaning a severe snowstorm, was invented in Estherville, Iowa around 1860. *Driveway*, *halter*, and *amazement* are also terms of United States origin.

New words are continually flowing into "United States English." Currently, the two greatest influences seem to be technology and slang. The space program has introduced such words as *launch pad*, *liftoff*, and *spacecraft*. Words from other technologies are *tape deck*, *cyberspace, pager, nuclear accelerator*, and *turbo-charged*. Slang words are usually only appropriate in casual speech and not in writing.

You might tell a friend she is wearing a cute dress, but if you were describing a scene for a book review, you would have to choose a more formal adjective. The reason for this choice is that slang words are often not precise in their meanings. If you walked into a hardware store and asked for some "stuff" for building a doghouse, the clerk would not know what you wanted: and if you told a policeman you had been "ripped," he would not know whether you had been robbed, if you were angry, or if your clothes had been torn.

For language to be effective, both the speaker and the listener must agree upon the meaning they use. However, you do not have to be a student of linguistics to communicate effectively.

Complete these activities.

1.19   Read a page or two of a newspaper or articles on a news website.

a.   Pick out several words that come from slang. (The sports section is a good place to find these terms.)

_____

_____

_____

_____

b.   Now turn to a different section and pick out several words that seem to come from technology.

_____

_____

_____

_____

c.   Why do you think words were invented for technical things?

_____

_____

_____

_____

_____

_____

_____

_____

_____

_____

_____

_____

_____

1.20 Choose a classmate and explain something to him, using nonsense for the key words. Example: This morning, before *glurk*, I *schlunked* to Bob's house because I had forgotten my *troister* there... After you have finished, have him tell you what he thought you said. Was it what you tried to express? Now have him do the explanation and you listen. Write some of the difficulties you encountered.

_____

_____

_____

_____

TEACHER CHECK _____ _____
initials   date

STANDARDIZATION OF LANGUAGE

You are probably beginning to wonder how we can understand literature that was written a century ago or even one generation ago, considering all the forces that change language. You may have begun to discover the answer to this problem yourself during your last exercise. If each person made up words to suit himself, no one would understand what anyone else was saying. The solution, then, is to have rules. Grammar is the set of rules that attempts to make English usage standard.

Of course, no set of rules is any good unless all the players know these rules. For this reason, the moveable type printing press (invented by Johann Gutenberg in 1454) had a great effect on the **standardization** of language. Books no longer had to be copied by hand, making many more books available to many more people.

| Gutenberg printing press

As a result, more people were able to observe how the educated writers of their day used the language and they, too, began to write and to speak in this way. Not long after this invention, scholars began to write down some of these habits of good writing in the form of grammatical rules. Thus, although living languages do and must change, their grammar makes sure that each generation will be able to understand the next.

Answer true or false.

1.21 _____ Unlike *dead* languages, *living* languages actually have no rules.

1.22 _____ The invention of the printing press made reading material more available.

1.23 _____ We would communicate more effectively if we could all make up our own grammar.

1.24 _____ We will probably have the same slang words in fifty years as we do now.

1.25 _____ Before the invention of the printing press, books were copied by hand.

TEACHER CHECK _____ _____
                        initials   date

SPELLING

In this section you will study some easily misspelled words. You may find writing any difficult words helpful.

Spelling Words-1		
absence	primitive	believe
accommodate	procedure	business
acknowledge	anxious	repetition
acquire	apparent	independent
aggressive	height	argument
existence	intelligence	grammar
familiar	benefited	government
finally	restaurant	athlete
foreign	receive	fulfill
personally	proceed	

Complete these activities.

1.26   Beside each word, write its part of speech (i.e. noun, verb, adjective).

a. absence _____   b. accommodate _____

c. acknowledge _____   d. acquire _____

e. aggressive _____   f. existence _____

g. familiar _____   h. finally _____

i. foreign _____   j. personally _____

k. primitive _____   l. privilege _____

m. procedure _____   n. anxious _____

o. apparent _____

1.27   Arrange these words in alphabetical order.

height	receive	repetition	government
intelligence	proceed	independent	athlete
benefited	believe	argument	fulfill
restaurant	business	grammar	

a. _____   i. _____

b. _____   j. _____

c. _____   k. _____

d. _____   l. _____

e. _____   m. _____

f. _____   n. _____

g. _____   o. _____

h. _____

ABC   **Ask your teacher to give you a practice spelling test of Spelling Words-1.** Restudy the words you missed.

TEACHER CHECK _____ _____

initials   date

Review the material in this section in preparation for the Self Test. The Self Test will check your mastery of this particular section. The items missed on this Self Test will indicate specific areas where restudy is needed for mastery.

SELF TEST 1

Define these terms (each answer, 4 points).

1.01 linguistics _____

_____

1.02 archaic _____

_____

1.03 assimilate _____

_____

1.04 unabridged _____

_____

1.05 derive _____

_____

Answer true or false (each answer, 1 point).

1.06 _____ German is a "dead" language.

1.07 _____ English has changed very little since the time of the King James Version of the Bible.

1.08 _____ Latin has no new words.

1.09 _____ The Normans conquered the English in 1066 but let them keep their language.

1.010 _____ Chaucer showed England that their language need not be considered vulgar.

1.011 _____ The etymology section in the dictionary is found in brackets.

1.012 _____ A people's language and their culture go together.

1.013 _____ Slang words are usually acceptable in writing.

1.014 _____ English in the United States does not include many foreign words.

1.015 _____ The word *lift-off* probably originated in the fifteenth century.

Match these items (each answer, 2 points).

1.016	_____ the study of word origins	a.	archaic
1.017	_____ rarely used in writing	b.	standard English
1.018	_____ invented the printing press	c.	Gutenberg
1.019	_____ rules for speaking and writing	d.	grammar
1.020	_____ a word from technology	e.	assimilate
1.021	_____ a language whose grammar never changes	f.	etymology
1.022	_____ what written English should be	g.	doth
1.023	_____ helped spread and develop language	h.	slang
1.024	_____ outdated words	i.	John Wycliffe
1.025	_____ words no longer in use	j.	trade
1.026	_____ an archaic word	k.	Sanskrit
		l.	obsolete
		m.	King James Version
		n.	radar

Answer these questions (each answer, 5 points).

1.027 How did the invention of the printing press aid in the standardization of language?

_____

_____

_____

_____

1.028 What is the function of slang?

_____

_____

_____

_____

1.029 Explain the difference between a *living* and a *dead* language.

_____

_____

_____

_____

_____

_____

_____

54 / 67		SCORE _____	TEACHER _____ _____
			initials date

ABC **Take your spelling test of Spelling Words-1.**

2. GOOD GRAMMAR MAKES SENSE

Babies are not born with the ability to speak and write. They have to learn it. We can hardly imagine not thinking in words; but if we did not have words, we might think in pictures. Pretend that you are a baby and that you have had certain memorable experiences with a particularly frightening object, such as a hot fireplace, that you would prefer to avoid in the future. You must develop the ability to arrange certain facts in your mind. You know that the terrible fireplace lies directly between you and your favorite toy. You know that, in order to get to the toy, you must cross in front of the fireplace, both on the way to get the toy and on the way back. You also know that the fireplace does not burn when the sun shines through the east window. What do you do? To us speaking people the answer is simple—you must get your toy in the morning. If you could not think in words, the solution would be much more difficult to come up with; and if you did figure it out, it would be almost impossible to explain to another youngster.

What grammar does for us is to provide *habits of thinking*. In other words, the rules of grammar give us a *system* for connecting our thoughts in a logical way. Babies have no system of putting their thoughts together. Each time they try to work out a problem, they have to *rediscover* a way to make sense of life through mental pictures. Even if a baby did figure out how to avoid the hot fireplace, this deduction would not help them learn to also avoid the electric coffee pot, which was hot in the mornings and in the evenings, but not at noon.

Fortunately, we do not have to rediscover the system for putting our basic thoughts together clearly each time we speak or write. We only have to follow the rules of grammar. Developing the habit of using good grammar is important because very often, poor grammar makes poor sense.

In this section you will be investigating some common grammatical pitfalls and how to avoid them. You will learn how to identify and to correct sentences using double negatives, dangling modifiers, faulty person and number, and faulty subject-verb agreement. You will also learn to spell some easily misspelled words.

SECTION OBJECTIVES

Review these objectives. When you have completed this section, you should be able to:

5. Spell new words correctly.
6. Identify and correct sentences with double negatives.
7. Identify and correct sentences with dangling modifiers.
8. Identify and correct sentences faulty in person and number.
9. Identify and correct sentences faulty in subject and verb agreement.

THE DOUBLE NEGATIVE

The double negative occurs as the result of attaching two negative *modifiers* to the verb of a sentence.

- **Example**:   I *haven't no* quarter.

The problem with the double negative is that each negative modifier tends to cancel out the other and make the sentence a positive statement. The sentence, "I haven't no quarter," actually means, "I have a quarter," because if you haven't no quarter, then you must have a quarter. Think of the sentence as if it were one side of a coin or the other. It must be either "heads" or "tails" just as the sentence must be either positive or negative. Each time you turn the coin over, you get the other side of the coin. If it is "heads" and you turn it over, then it will show "tails." In the same way, when you start out with a positive statement, such as "I have a quarter," and turn it over by using the negative word *no* instead of *a*, the sentence becomes negative. "I have got no quarter" is a negative statement. If you begin with you coin showing "heads" and you turn it over *twice*, it will show "heads" again. The same is true with the sentence. If you use one negative, the sentence becomes negative; but if you use two negatives, the sentence becomes positive again. (Naturally, however, two or more positives will not make a negative.) If you want to correct a double negative, all you have to do is remove one of the negatives.

- **Wrong**: I *haven't no* quarter. (two negatives)
- **Right**: I *have no* quarter. (one negative)
- **Right**: I *haven't* a quarter. (one negative)

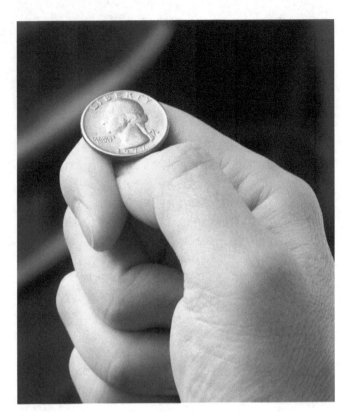

| Heads or Tails?

While avoiding double negatives, you also need to watch for *implied* negatives. Because the words *hardly* and *scarcely* are negative in meaning, they should not be used with other negatives.

- **Wrong**: I *can't hardly* understand him. (two negatives)
- **Right**: I can *hardly* understand him. (one negative)
- **Wrong**: Bob *won't scarcely* have time to catch the bus. (two negatives)
- **Right**: Bob will *scarcely* have time to catch the bus. (one negative)

Rewrite these sentences.

2.1 We haven't been to no ball games in over a month.

_____

2.2 Without getting an extra day I can't hardly see how I finish the job.

_____

2.3 Jim shouldn't have never gone without you.

_____

2.4 I can't sing very well neither.

_____

2.5 I'm tired of being captain because nobody never does nothing.

_____

2.6 We can't hardly get along without Tom.

_____

2.7 You haven't seen nothing yet!

_____

2.8 The time comes in a man's life when he doesn't want no help.

_____

2.9 Unless everybody shows up, our plans don't hardly matter.

_____

2.10 The water isn't scarcely enough for the three of us.

_____

DANGLING MODIFIERS

To avoid confusion, a modifier is placed near the word it modifies. A modifier can be a word, a phrase, or a clause. Dangling modifiers are either attached to the wrong word or to no word at all. The result is usually humorous confusion about what the sentence is saying. Three basic kinds of dangling modifiers exist.

Dangling participles. A _participle_ is a verb that also has the properties of an adjective; it functions as an adjective, or does the work of an adjective.

■ **Example**: _Waving_ frantically, he flagged down the train.

Waving is the participle; it modifies the word _he_. _Waving frantically_ is the participial phrase.

An introductory participial phrase will modify the wrong word or no word. A dangling participle will modify the wrong word or no word.

- **Wrong**: Being a disaster, *John* thought the flood would make a good news story.

- **Right**: John thought that, being a disaster, *the flood* would make a good news story.

In the preceding sentence being a disaster is the participial phrase. Obviously, the disaster being discussed is *the flood*, not *John*. Therefore, *the flood*, not *John* should come after *being a disaster*.

- **Wrong**: Walking the gangplank, *the sharks* terrified Jack.

- **Right**: Walking the gangplank, *Jack* was terrified by the sharks.

We all know that sharks do not walk the gangplanks on ships; people do. Thus, Jack or another person's name should follow the participial phrase, *walking the gangplank*.

- **Wrong**: Driving to the lake, an *owl* flew across the road.

- **Right**: Driving to the lake, *we* saw an owl fly across the road.

Owls do not *drive* to the lake or anywhere else.

| Walking the gangplank, the sharks terrified Jack.

Rewrite these following sentences.

2.11 Running down the street, John's ice cream fell in the mud.

_____

2.12 Looking through the library, several books on horses can be found.

_____

2.13 Flipping through the telephone directory, the name he wanted was found.

_____

2.14 Eating breakfast one morning, the idea came to him.

_____

2.15 Picking up his pencil, Tom's shoes, he noticed, were untied.

_____

Dangling infinitives. An _infinitive_ is a verb form preceded by _to_. An infinitive can function as a noun, an adjective, or an adverb.

- **Examples**: to run, to consider, to read, to drive

A dangling infinitive modifier is separated from the word it modifies. An introductory adjective infinitive will modify the subject following the comma.

- **Wrong**: To be well cooked, _you_ must bake the chicken an hour.

- **Right**: To be well cooked, _the chicken_ must be baked for an hour.

The _chicken_ is to be baked, not _you_.

- **Wrong**: To be informed, _the rules_ should be read thoroughly.

- **Right**: To be informed, _one_ should read the rules thoroughly.

One should be informed. _Rule_s cannot be informed.

 Write an X by the correct sentence.

2.16 _____ To eat a tangerine, the peeling should first be removed.

_____ To eat a tangerine, you should first remove the peeling.

2.17 _____ To be a farmer these days, a person is required to have a knowledge of chemistry.

_____ To be a farmer these days, a knowledge of chemistry is required.

2.18 _____ To catch the bus on time, I would have to run five blocks.

_____ To catch the bus on time, running five blocks would be necessary.

2.19 _____ To see clearly underwater, goggles must be worn.

_____ To see clearly underwater, one must wear goggles.

2.20 _____ To understand the history professor, his new book ought to be read.

_____ To understand the history professor, you ought to read his new book.

Dangling elliptical clauses. An elliptical clause is one in which one or more words have been omitted.

- **Example**: _While idling_, the car uses less gasoline.

The implied words in this elliptical clause are _the car_. (While _the car_ is idling, the car uses less gasoline.) Using an elliptical clause is not wrong as long as the clause modifies correctly. When it does not, it is considered a dangling elliptical clause.

- **Wrong**: While idling, less gas is being used by the car.

- **Right**: While idling, the car uses less gas.

The _car_ idles; the _gas_ does not.

- **Wrong**: When little girls, _anteaters_ at the zoo fascinated my sister and me.

| When little girls, anteaters at the zoo fascinated my sister and me.

- **Right**: When little girls, _my sister and I_ were fascinated by the anteaters at the zoo.

The little girl and her sister were never anteaters at the zoo.

Rewrite these sentences.

2.21 While jogging, my shoelaces come untied.

_____

2.22 If adopted, I hope my plan will lead to lower taxes.

_____

2.23 When three, my grandfather taught me to play checkers.

_____

2.24 When reading, my eyes grow tired.

_____

2.25 If late, mother would punish me.

_____

SHIFT IN PERSON

A shift in person within a sentence can confuse the reader about the subject of the sentence.

- **Wrong**: If *you* come from a happy family, *one* should be thankful.

- **Right**: If *you* come from a happy family, *you* should be thankful.

- **Right**: If *one* comes from a happy family, *he* should be thankful.

In the preceding incorrect sentence, the writer shifts from the second person, *you*, to the third person, *one*. Although such shifts are unintentional, grammatically they indicate that the *you* and the *one* refer to different people.

- **Wrong**: When a *person* has a job to do, *you* ought to do it.

- **Right**: When a *person* has a job to do, *he* ought to do it.

Note: *He* can be used with such words as *one*, *a man*, *a person*, or *anybody*.

Circle the correct word in these sentences.

2.26   When a boy reaches high school age, (he, you) must consider the future.

2.27   If (one, you) had to choose his favorite flavor, he might take forever.

2.28   I wish a person could relax whenever (he, you) wanted.

2.29   If a guy lets his mother buy his clothes for him sometimes, a. (he, you) b. (is, are) sure to have a nice wardrobe.

2.30   One always has time for the things a. (he, you) b. (wants, want) to do.

SHIFT IN NUMBER

A pronoun and its *antecedent* should always agree in number. Use a *singular pronoun* to refer to such antecedents as *person, woman, man, one, anyone, anybody, someone, somebody, everyone, everybody, each*, or *neither*. Remember that an antecedent is the noun or pronoun to which a pronoun refers.

- **Wrong**: *Each* of us agreed to carry *our own* weight.

- **Right**: *Each* of us agreed to carry *his own* weight.

Each refers to a single individual and *our* refers to more than one. Two or more antecedents joined by *and* must use a plural pronoun.

- **Wrong**: John *and* his friend did *his* homework. (unless both worked on John's homework)

- **Right**: John and his friend did their homework.

Antecedents joined by *nor* or *or* must use a singular pronoun.

- **Wrong**: Neither John *nor* his friend did *their* homework.

- **Right**: Neither John *nor* his friend did *his* homework.

A collective noun may use a singular pronoun or a plural pronoun, depending on its meaning.

- **Wrong**: The *jury* has reached *their* verdict.

- **Right**: The *jury* has reached *its* verdict. (acting together; a verdict is reached by the group)

- **Wrong**: The *jury* has not turned in *its* vote.

- **Right**: The jury have not turned in their votes. (acting as individuals; a vote is cast by each juror)

Rewrite these sentences.

2.31 In this snowstorm nobody could find their way home.

_____

_____

2.32 The team has elected their new captain.

_____

_____

2.33 Neither Mary nor her friend wanted their picture taken.

_____

_____

2.34 Mary and her friend did her best to hide from the photographer.

_____

_____

2.35 The person who left their banana peel on my chair had better come and get it.

_____

_____

2.36 One needs a tractor to plow their field.

_____

_____

2.37 Anyone wishing to teach Sunday school should bring their Bible to church next Sunday.

_____

_____

2.38 Will somebody please say what they mean?

_____

_____

2.39 I would prefer that Robert and John found his own ride home.

_____

_____

2.40 If the Boy Scouts work hard, it will earn merit badges.

_____

_____

SUBJECT-VERB AGREEMENT

The subject and the verb of a sentence should *both* be either singular or plural.

- **Wrong**: *Math* and *science is* all I need.

- **Right**: *Math* and *science are* all I need.

- **Wrong**: *Neither* of us *are* ready.

- **Right**: Neither of us *is* ready.

Circle the correct word in these sentences.

2.41 Ten miles (is, are) too far to run.

2.42 Neither of us (is, are) driving to Canada.

2.43 Among the five of us, only two of us (is, are) cooks.

2.44 (Is, Are) everybody having a good time?

2.45 All that we have (is, are) God's.

SHIFT IN MOOD AND TENSE

Two types of shifts can cause problems in written or spoken English. These shifts can occur in *mood* or in *tense.*

Shift in mood. The *mood* of a verb refers to the way that the action or state of being is stated. In English, the three moods of a verb are *indicative*, *subjunctive*, and *imperative.*

The *indicative* mood asks a question or states a fact.

Examples:

- Is the city far away?

- The cat is beautiful.

- The African camel has only one hump.

The *subjunctive* mood expresses an opinion contrary to fact, usually in the form of a doubt or a wish.

Examples:

- He smiles as if he *were* already president.

- I wish I *were* tall enough to play basketball.

- If I *were* you, I would come back now.

The subjunctive is used after such words as *as if, as though, I request* (suggest, ask, move...) *that*, and other expressions contrary to fact.

Examples:

- I request that I *be* excused early.

- She acts as though she *were* deaf.

- They asked that we *be* quieter.

The *imperative* mood expresses a command or a plea.

Examples:

- *Shut* the door!

- Please *stop talking* when the bell rings.

Study the following examples of shifts in mood and their corrected forms.

- **Shift**: If his dream *came* true and he *was* the richest man in the world, I believe he would be very unhappy.

- **Correct**: If his dream *came* true and he *were* the richest man in the world, I believe he would be very unhappy.

- **Shift**: *Shut* the door and you *ought to be seated*.

- **Correct**: *Shut* the door and *be* seated.

| "I wish I were tall enough to play basketball."

✎ **Match each sentence with its mood.** You may use an answer more than once.

2.46 _____ I wish I were a good swimmer.

2.47 _____ He can always stay home.

2.48 _____ Leave that alone.

2.49 _____ If I were you, I would not do that.

a. subjunctive

b. imperative

c. indicative

Write the correct verb form for each sentence. Avoid confusing shifts in mood.

2.50 If you were serious about studying _____ wasting time.

(then stop, you would stop)

2.51 Sit up and _____ attention.

(pay, you ought to pay)

2.52 Even if some boys did climb the tree, _____ try it!

(don't you, I don't want you to)

Shift in tense. A shift in the tense of a sentence makes a reader wonder *what* is happening *when*.

- **Wrong**: Susan *dashed* across the room and *begins* to play the violin.

- **Right**: Susan *dashed* across the room and *began* to play the violin.

- **Right**: Susan *dashes* across the room and *begins* to play the violin.

Circle the correct word in these sentences.

2.53 Not much time had passed before Paul (starts, started) to feel ashamed.

2.54 Next fall, Marion (begins, will begin) art lessons.

2.55 Wilber (thinks, thought) a moment before he gave his answer.

2.56 No other chicken that lived in the whole county (is, was) as loyal as Bert.

2.57 Hurrying to the airport, Sam (forgets, forgot) which way he should have turned.

SPELLING

The following list contains several frequently misspelled words.

Spelling Words-2		
unnecessary	environment	ninth
dinosaurs	embarrass	niece
grammatical	doesn't	necessary
usually	twelfth	misspelled
vacuum	sophomore	dissatisfied
omission	strength	discipline
optimistic	tendency	curiosity
parallel	occurrence	deceive
perceive	occasionally	desperate
exaggerate	nowadays	definite

unnecessary	omission	environment	strength	ninth	discipline
dinosaurs	optimistic	embarrass	tendency	niece	curiosity
grammatical	parallel	doesn't	occurrence	necessary	deceive
usually	perceive	twelfth	occasionally	misspelled	desperate
vacuum	exaggerate	sophomore	nowadays	dissatisfied	definite

Complete these activities.

2.58 Complete these sentences with the appropriate words from the first two columns
of Spelling Words-2 list above.

a. I don't mean to _____ , but I am the strongest person in the whole world.

b. Not inviting old Aunt Mumby was a serious _____ .

c. I can _____ that you are an intelligent girl.

d. Lines of longitude and latitude are not _____ .

e. Mother lets me run the _____ cleaner.

f. You might say that Job was an _____ man.

g. I _____ eat dinner by six o'clock.

h. This here sentence are not _____ .

i. Owning fifty-seven pairs of shoes is _____ .

j. Many years ago _____ roamed the earth.

2.59 Using the entire list of Spelling Words-2, find the words with double consonants and divide
each one into syllables.

a. _____   b. _____

c. _____   d. _____

e. _____   f. _____

g. _____   h. _____

i. _____   j. _____

k. _____   l. _____

ABC **Ask your teacher to give you a practice spelling test of Spelling Words-2.** Restudy the
words you missed.

TEACHER CHECK _____ _____

initials   date

Review the material in this section in preparation for the Self Test. The Self Test will check your mastery of this particular section as well as your knowledge of the previous section.

SELF TEST 2

Circle the correct word in these sentences (each answer, 2 points).

2.01   Sunday (is, is not) hardly the proper day to start a new job.

2.02   Did anybody remember to bring (his, their) lunch today?

2.03   Both of us (is, are) going to be late for school.

2.04   I don't find (anything, nothing) wrong with the newspaper.

2.05   The club's membership (is, are) now well over fifty.

2.06   Because Bill had only five minutes to get to work, he (forgets, forgot) his lunch.

2.07   Doing twenty pushups (are, is) enough for me.

2.08   Dad and Dr. Smith (has, have) played golf all day.

2.09   Neither of us (is, are) entering the contest.

2.010 Every one of us cannot have (his, our) way.

Rewrite these sentences (each answer, 4 points).

2.011 Gulping down his breakfast, a piece of toast stuck in his throat.

_____

2.012 After many hours of prayer, the problem was resolved in Tom's mind.

_____

2.013 When cleaning, the dust gets in my eyes.

_____

2.014 Unrolling his sleeping bag, the night was strangely quiet.

_____

2.015 One should read their assignment in the textbook.

_____

Write an X by the correct sentence (each answer, 2 points).

2.016 _____ a. Be quiet, and you ought to be considerate of others.

_____ b. You ought to be considerate of others and keep quiet.

2.017 _____ a. When one becomes a professor, you should not play favorites.

_____ b. When one becomes a professor, one should not play favorites.

2.018 _____ a. Glancing at his watch, he saw the time had run out.

_____ b. Glancing at his watch, the time had run out.

2.019 _____ a. Finishing his lesson, the book was laid aside

_____ b. Finishing his lesson, he laid his book aside.

2.020 _____ a. You are talking as if I were your last hope.

_____ b. You are talking as if I am you last hope.

2.021 _____ a. When telling stories, there is always excitement in the old man's voice.

_____ b. When telling stories, the old man always spoke with excitement.

2.022 _____ a. If there is twenty mules, each with its own pack of one hundred pounds, how many trips is necessary to transport one ton?

_____ b. If there are twenty mules, each with its own pack of one hundred pounds, how many trips are necessary to transport one ton?

2.023 _____ a. Sometimes I can hardly read my own handwriting.

_____ b. Sometimes I can't hardly read my own handwriting.

2.024 _____ a. Wilber wouldn't give his address to nobody.

_____ b. Wilber wouldn't give his address to anybody.

2.025 _____ a. While prancing through the meadow, a meteor startled the lamb.

_____ b. While prancing through the meadow, the lamb was startled by the meteor.

Complete the following sentences by writing the correct word from this list on each line. Some words may be used more than once (each answer, 2 points).

is	was	some	he	have
are	your	his	no	their
am	you	were	any	one

2.026 For this position, there _____ two requirements.

2.027 I don't have _____ idea what you are saying.

2.028 Neither Robert nor I _____ farmed before.

2.029 Each person must bring _____ own lunch.

2.030 One never knows what _____ is expected to wear.

2.031 It was not until spring that the boys _____ well.

2.032 Two times one is two, but the sum of two plus one _____ three.

2.033 Nobody finished _____ test in time.

2.034 Three of us _____ all it took to push the car.

2.035 When I was little, if one of us cried, we _____ likely to make fun of him.

Complete these statements (each answer, 3 points).

2.036 The study of languages is referred to as _____ .

2.037 In 1066 A.D. the English were conquered by the a. _____ , who spoke

b. _____ .

2.038 The study of word origins is known as _____ .

2.039 The two greatest influences on language today seem to be technology and

_____ .

2.040 The invention of the a. _____ by b. _____ helped

spread and standardize language.

2.041 Two men who were responsible for translating the Bible, or parts of it, into English were

a. _____ and b. _____ .

2.042 A contemporary, changing language still in popular use is known as a

a. _____ language; a language that is spoken and written only by scholars is called a

b. _____ language.

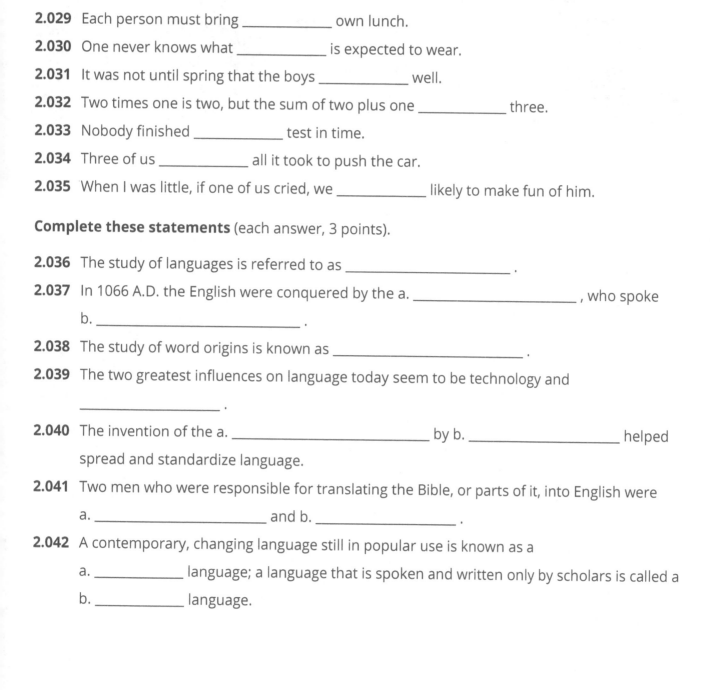

90 / 113   **SCORE** _____   **TEACHER** _____ _____
initials   date

Take your spelling test of Spelling Words-2.

3. AN ORAL REPORT SHOULD BE ORGANIZED

Because nearly everyone speaks much more than they write, the ability to speak well can be an even greater asset than the ability to write well. If somebody were to hand you a transcript (a written record) of every word you had spoken over a period of one month, it would probably be as thick as a large city telephone directory. However, if you were then to start reading through it, you would probably be embarrassed by how little you actually said in proportion to how much you spoke. Although you cannot be expected to keep silent unless you have something splendid to say, you could learn to communicate your ideas and feelings with more precision if you were more aware of some of the rules of effective speaking.

The mind is constantly generating ideas, remembering facts and feelings, responding to questions, and creating daydreams. A person trying to read the transcript of your thoughts might become confused about what led you from one particular idea to the next. Sometimes, even when you try to analyze your own patterns of thinking, you can find no logic to them. Thus, the problem you face whenever you try to write or to speak is how to focus your thoughts into patterns somebody else can understand.

| "I said all that?"

In this section, you will learn more about organizing material so that you will be able to present organized reports and papers. You will learn about a method of organization called the "pentad." You will learn the functions of a report. You will study style and effective speech. You will also study some more spelling words.

SECTION OBJECTIVES

Review these objectives. When you have completed this section, you should be able to:

5. Spell new words correctly.
10. Restate the elements of the pentad.
11. Explain the functions of an oral report.
12. Explain various elements in preparing and presenting an oral report.

VOCABULARY

Study these words to enhance your learning success in this section.

appropriate (u prō´ prē it). *adj*. Suitable.

inflect (in flekt´). *verb*. To vary the pitch of the voice.

pentad (pen´ tad). *noun*. A group or a series of five things.

jargon (jär´ gun). *noun*. Specialized or technical language.

ORGANIZING INFORMATION

At the end of this section, you will be asked to prepare a brief oral report on a topic of your choice. The most difficult problem you will face is how to begin. One helpful tool for those attempting to focus their thinking into logical patterns is called the **pentad**. It is composed of five areas about which the speaker can ask himself before he begins to organize his report.

These questions resemble those you have learned that a news story should answer: *What, Who, Where, When, How,* and *Why*.

1. What action (What?)
   - What is it?
   - What happened?
   - What will or could happen?
2. What agent (Who?)
   - What king of agent is the actor (person, organization, social trend)?
   - What did it?
   - Who did it?
3. What setting (Where? and When?)
   - What is the scene?
   - Where did it (or will it or could it) happen?
4. What means (How?)
   - How did the agent accomplish the action?
5. What purpose (Why?)
   - What was the agent's motive?

Even before you begin to use the pentad, you must decide on a topic. Your topic should be something that interests you and something about which you have some special knowledge. Let us say that you decide to report on the hike you took with your family to the bottom of the Grand Canyon. Now you are ready to start taking notes using the pentad.

What action (What?)

- *What is it?* The hike you took with your family to the bottom of the Grand Canyon.

- *What happened?* Here, you can jot down a few details about how you prepared for the trip, any incidents along the way, and about the hike itself.

Who or what acted as the agent (Who?)

- *Who did it*? The "agents" are, of course, you and your family. You can write down descriptions of the members of your family and yourself. You can include how you all felt about the trip and what each person said or did that was memorable.

What setting (Where? When?)

- *What is the scene*? You might want to include three scenes: your home, getting ready for the trip, the drive to the Grand Canyon, and the canyon itself. This setting would mean that you would also include three different "whens."

By what means (How?)

■ *How did the agent accomplish the action*?
Did you backpack? Did you camp? How did
you prepare for the trip? How did you endure
the long hike? Be sure to make a note of any
unusual incidents and how you and your
family reacted to them.

For what purpose (Why?)

■ *What were the agent's motives?* What made
you all decide to go to the Grand Canyon and
take on such a strenuous adventure?
If you think the trip was a success, say why
you think so.

If you have answered all these questions with a
moderate amount of detail, you probably have
all the facts you need to write your report. How
much you elaborate on these details depends
upon how long your report is to be. In this case,
you should try to include enough material to fill
five minutes. Be careful not to make your report
much shorter or much longer.

Identify the elements of the pentad in the following passage from Genesis.

> *In the beginning God created the heaven and the earth.*
> *And the earth was without form, and void; and darkness*
> *was upon the face of the deep. And the Spirit of God moved*
> *upon the face of the waters.*
> *And God said, Let there be light: and there was light.*
> *And God saw the light, that it was good: and God*
> *divided the light from the darkness.*
> *And God called the light Day, and the darkness*
> *He called Night. And the evening and the morning were*
> *the first day.*

3.1   What action? _____

3.2   Who or what acted as an agent? _____

3.3   What setting? _____

3.4   By what means? _____

3.5   For what purpose? _____

Now that you have limited the length of your report, you need to decide upon its function. You may choose the function of the report from several categories:

- **Exposition**: a presentation of information, such as a travel log.

- **Process and analysis**: a step-by-step examination of how something works.

- **Definition**: a precise statement of factual description.

- **Persuasion**: a presentation of an opinion and the reasons behind it, designed to convince a neutral person of its validity.

- **Expression**: a presentation designed mainly for entertainment. It may be humorous, satirical, or beautifully descriptive.

Using the example of the hike down the Grand Canyon, let us say the you decide upon *expression* as the function of your report since you are not enough of an expert on hiking or the Grand Canyon to use *definition* or *process* and *analysis*. A factual exposition of the hike would not be very exciting and you may not see any advantage in using persuasion to tell people that you had a good time.

Now that you know what you want to say and how you want to say it, you need to *organize* your material. Your report should have a *beginning*, a *middle*, and an *end*. Perhaps this statement sounds too simple, so let us say that your report needs a *thesis*, a *main body*, and a *conclusion*.

The thesis is probably the most important element of your report. In it you will introduce the most important element of your report—the purpose or the direction of your report. The thesis should capture the attention of the audience and make them want to hear the rest. A thesis for your report on the Grand Canyon hike might read:

> *Braving the sweltering heat of the days and the icy snap of the desert nights and*

> *dodging daredevil pack mules, my family and I discovered that a hike to the bottom of the Grand Canyon can be a test of endurance as well as an exploration of incredible natural beauty.*

Having written the beginning of your report, you should have a fairly good idea about what you need to say in the main body and conclusion. Since the thesis is a statement based upon certain information, the main body of the report should contain that information. A thesis not backed by corresponding information resembles a magician who promises to pull a rabbit out of a hat but never does. The thesis sets up certain expectations in the audience that the main body of the report must resolve. The main body of the report on the Grand Canyon hike should include descriptions of how hot and how cold the weather was. Some time should be spent on the incident with the daredevil pack mules and other hardships. Also, some attention should be given to a few of the beautiful sights along the trail.

The conclusion of a five-minute report need not go into a lengthy summary of the information in the main body. The conclusion should only be a short statement or comment that expresses the general attitude of the report. The conclusion will probably draw heavily from the *why* part of the pentad. You might take the opportunity here to say, for example, if the hike down the canyon was worth the effort.

> *As the four of us lay sprawled out on the grass beside the car, I remember thinking that we looked like a crew of castaways just rescued by the Coast Guard. Although we were glad to be back to "civilization," I think we were a little sad the adventure was over. "Maybe," I thought, "even in a bunch of city folk from Detroit like us, the pioneer spirit is still alive."*

After you have taken all your notes and decided on what kind of organization you intend to use, you will have to discard some of the information you have gathered so that your report will flow smoothly. Remember that you will be giving the report orally and unless you move briskly from one point or incident to the next, your audience will become bored.

Although you may not have said everything you think is important about a certain point, you should move on to the next point while your audience is still interested.

Define these words.

3.6   thesis _____

_____

3.7   process and analysis _____

_____

3.8   means _____

_____

3.9   exposition _____

_____

3.10 purpose _____

_____

Answer true or false.

3.11 _____   When writing a report, you must include everything in your notes.

3.12 _____   A persuasion report should be factual and convincing.

3.13 _____   The main body of the report contains support for the thesis.

3.14 _____   Your audience will not be bored if you say everything you know about each point in your report.

USING LANGUAGE

Even the best ideas in the world spoken with the greatest enthusiasm can only be made up of words, and words mean different things to different people. While you are organizing your report, be sure to keep in mind the audience to which you will be speaking. You must be certain that both the subject, and the language are **appropriate** to your audience. You would not, for example, want to give a *process-analysis* report on sky diving to members of a nursing home or a *persuasion* report on the evils of war to the American Legion. Even though you might enjoy giving such reports, you must be considerate of your audience. You must also be careful to use language that is meaningful to your audience. If you wanted to talk about electronics to a group of people untrained in the field, you should not use such technical **jargon** as *diodes*, *resistors*, and *capacitors* without explaining what they mean. Using slang words in a speech is generally not a good idea; but if you use them, be sure that your audience is likely to understand what they mean. If you think they will not be familiar with certain slang words, do not try to explain them; simply leave them out of your speech.

The *style* of your report must be *appropriate* to the subject matter and to the audience. If you were giving a report on the operations of a funeral home, a light, humorous style would not be appropriate. If you were giving a report to your friends about a school football game, you would probably use an informal style, omitting ten-syllable words when simpler words would do. After choosing a topic for your report, you should be thinking about the style you will need to use and deciding whether that style should be *formal*, *informal*, *humorous*, or *serious*.

Even if you remember nothing else about preparing a report, remember to use *precise* language. By saying only what you need to say to convey information, you save time and keep your audience's attention. If you ramble and use unnecessary words and phrases, your audience will be bored. Notice the difference between the following examples.

- **Sloppy**: <u>It is just my opinion, of course, but I think</u> pole-vaulting is certainly one of the most <u>pleasing to watch</u> and <u>hard things you can do</u> in <u>the sport</u> of track and field.

- **Better**: Pole-vaulting is one of the most beautiful and technically demanding events in track and field.

In the example of sloppy language, the under-lined words could be left out without detracting much from the content of the sentence. The opening words, *it is just my opinion*, of course, takes away any of the power the sentence might have had. An audience probably would not be interested in anything that was just one person's opinion. If what you have to say is

not likely to be applicable to anyone else, you have no business asking him to listen to it. If you wish to give your opinion, do so without apologizing and state your case as if any reasonable person might believe the same thing. In the sloppy example the word *certainly* would not be necessary if the writer had presented his opinion as if he were certain of the truth of his statement.

Pleasing to watch, hard things, and *you can do* are all imprecise phrases that require the audience to substitute mentally other words that communicate what the author probably means. We can understand what the writer is trying to say, but the language is wordy and awkward. Compare these phrases from the sloppy example with the more precise phrases from the better example. Instead of *pleasing to watch*, the writer uses beautiful; in place of *hard things*, he uses *technically demanding*. The better example creates a clearer picture, probably because its author had a clearer picture in his mind of what he wanted to say. *The sport of,* used in the sloppy example, is unnecessary because most people know that track and field is a sport and the pole-vaulting is a sporting event.

As you prepare your oral presentation, keep the mechanism of *statement* and *support* constantly in your mind. Whenever you make a statement, ask yourself if you are prepared to support it with *facts, explanations, or illustrations*. Unless you can provide the support, do not make the statement. If you say that most people in this country drive American cars, you should include the *statistics* upon which the statement is based. If you say that for mountain climbing, hiking boots are better for your feet than tennis shoes, you need to provide an explanation; and if you say that becoming a Christian has made you a happier person, you need to give an illustration (example) of what you mean.

Be careful to avoid *unsupportable* statements based only on prejudice or opinion.

- **Unsupportable**: Those big, ugly gas-hog automobiles are disgusting! Only a show-off would want one.

- **Supportable**: Full-sized cars are a drain on our nation's natural resources. They require more raw materials to manufacture and more fuel to keep running than smaller cars with the same seating capacity.

The first author cannot "prove" that big cars are disgusting, but the second author could probably find the facts to support his claim that big cars cost more to make and maintain than small cars that seat the same number of people. Finding supportive evidence for statements you make will give you a better chance of convincing your audience that what you say is true and will also help you construct a more *logical* argument.

Write an X by the more effective sentence.

3.15 _____ The president was a hot-headed authoritarian.

_____ The president sometimes made major decisions without the consent of his advisors.

3.16 _____ Classical music is much different from big band music.

_____ Classical music is much better than big band music.

3.17 _____ I had a swell time at Lake Mead.

_____ I caught three bass at Lake Mead.

3.18 _____ Now that I look back on it, I guess that last year at Grandma's place, I had the best Thanksgiving that I ever did have in all my life.

_____ Looking back on it, I believe Thanksgiving at Grandma's place last year was the best I ever had.

3.19 _____ The aspirin upset his stomach.

_____ The $C_9H_8O_4$ upset his stomach.

SPEAKING EFFECTIVELY

After you have prepared your report making sure that the organization is logical, the statements are carefully supported, the language is clear and precise, and the thesis and conclusion are powerful, you still do not know if your report will be a success until you have given it before an audience. Since the audience will be the judge of your report's quality, speak to the audience. Do not stare at your paper or at anything around the room while you talk.

Look at the audience. Eye contact is one of the most important elements of public speaking. When a speaker looks at you during a speech, you feel that they are personally concerned that you understand and appreciate what they are saying. If the speaker looks at the walls, you may not feel the necessity to pay attention to their speech.

Since you will be talking to people, you must give your report as if you have just thought it up and would like your audience to hear it. Try to make your voice sound "natural." Ordinarily, when you talk, your voice changes *pitch* and volume. Also, when you are making an important point, your voice emphasizes those words. Thus, when you give your report, do not speak in a monotone; allow your voice to be naturally **inflected**.

Because the audience will not think your report is good if they cannot hear you, be sure to speak out clearly. The technique for making yourself heard by everyone in the room is called *projection* because you project your voice to reach even the back of the room. Since people usually converse at close range, they sometimes get away with not *enunciating* (pronouncing words carefully). When you are in front of a group of people, however, you will hear them shuffling their feet, coughing, and even whispering to each other. All these things make it difficult for you, the speaker, to be heard.

Therefore, you must make a special effort to form your words carefully as you speak. Inexperienced speakers often make the mistake of speaking too rapidly. The more rapidly you talk, the harder you are to understand.

Because you are a human being and not a tape recorder, your audience will be looking at you; you will need to give them something to watch. You should stand up straight with your feet together. When you are making a point or describing something, you can direct the attention of the audience by using *gestures* for emphasis. The only "rule" for using gestures effectively is to not fold your arms or put your hands in your pockets. Let your hands move as they naturally would when you speak.

The best word of advice for you at this point is to have fun with your presentation. Get excited about your performance and let your excitement show. If your audience sees that you are interested in your report, they will be likely to be caught up in your enthusiasm and to enjoy your report even more.

| Always make eye contact.

Define these terms.

3.20 eye contact _____

_____

3.21 projection _____

_____

3.22 gesture _____

_____

3.23 pitch _____

_____

3.24 enunciate _____

_____

Complete this activity.

3.25 Write a report on a separate sheet or two of paper.

a. Choose one of the following topics and patterns or make up one of your own.

☐ *My Favorite Hobby*. You could write an exposition report about your hobby; for example, stamp collecting.

☐ *My Best Friend*. You might write an expression report about why this person is your best friend.

☐ *Why My Room Is Like Me*. You could write a process and analysis report, describing why your room at home reflects your personality. Be specific.

b. Use the pentad to outline and plan your report.

c. Write the report neatly. Your teacher may ask you to present your report orally.

TEACHER CHECK _____   _____
                              initials   date

SPELLING

The following list contains words with "silent letters." The words are common but because they are not spelled the way they sound, they are frequently misspelled.

	Spelling Words-3	
climb	knife	February
debt	knight	aisle
doubt	knot	island
thumb	calm	listen
sign	condemn	guess
ghost	hymn	answer
Wednesday	courtesy	mortgage
scene	solemn	muscle
lamb	palm	yacht
handsome	pneumonia	subtle

 Match these definitions with the correct words.

3.26	_____ sickness		a.	hymn
3.27	_____ crafty		b.	courtesy
3.28	_____ after January		c.	solemn
3.29	_____ surrounded by water		d.	palm
3.30	_____ hear		e.	pneumonia
3.31	_____ reply		f.	February
3.32	_____ money for a house		g.	sign
3.33	_____ boat		h.	island
3.34	_____ underside of hand		i.	listen
3.35	_____ song		j.	guess
3.36	_____ politeness		k.	answer
3.37	_____ sad		l.	mortgage
3.38	_____ estimate		m.	muscle
3.39	_____ strength		n.	aisle
3.40	_____ passageway		o.	yacht
			p.	subtle
			q.	thumb

Complete this activity.

3.41   Circle the spelling words in this puzzle. The words may be backwards or up and down.

```
T   B   E   D   O   O   E   K   E   N
O   C   O   N   D   E   M   N   A   C
T   H   U   M   B   D   O   I   Q   D
S   C   E   N   E   O   S   F   P   T
O   A   I   G   L   U   D   E   R   H
H   L   O   I   A   B   N   S   O   G
G   M   T   S   M   T   A   H   B   I
C   L   I   M   B   X   H   S   Z   N
O   Q   E   R   P   A   T   O   N   K
Y   A   D   S   E   N   D   E   W   Y
```

ABC **Ask your teacher to give you a practice spelling test of Spelling Words-3.** Restudy the words you missed.

TEACHER CHECK _____ _____
                       initials   date

Before you take this last Self Test, you may want to do one or more of these self checks.

1.   _____   Read the objectives. See if you can do them.
2.   _____   Restudy the material related to any objectives that you cannot do.
3.   _____   Use the **SQ3R** study procedure to review the material:
       a. **S**can the sections.
       b. **Q**uestion yourself.
       c. **R**ead to answer your questions.
       d. **R**ecite the answers to yourself.
       e. **R**eview areas you did not understand.
4.   _____   Review all vocabulary, activities, and Self Tests, writing a correct answer for every wrong answer.

SELF TEST 3

Answer true or false (each answer, 1 point).

3.01 _____ The actor-agent of a pentad refers only to human beings.

3.02 _____ An exposition is a creative presentation.

3.03 _____ The main body of the report should contain supportive information.

3.04 _____ The conclusion should include a long summary statement.

3.05 _____ The subject of a speech should be appropriate to its audience.

3.06 _____ Using slang words in public speaking is generally acceptable.

3.07 _____ Not all public speeches should be formal.

3.08 _____ Audiences are impressed favorably with speakers who gaze at the ceiling.

3.09 _____ Details are only important in a factual report.

Match these terms (each answer, 2 points).

3.010 _____ How?

3.011 _____ statement of purpose and direction

3.012 _____ should be convincing

3.013 _____ the middle of the report

3.014 _____ technical language

3.015 _____ method of organization

3.016 _____ Why?

3.017 _____ presentation designed for entertainment

3.018 _____ speaking clearly

3.019 _____ noninflected speech

a. appropriate

b. enunciation

c. by what means

d. pentad

e. for what purpose

f. main body

g. jargon

h. persuasion

i. monotone

j. expression

k. thesis

l. process

Define these terms (each answer, 4 points).

3.020 thesis _____

_____

3.021 etymology _____

_____

3.022 grammar _____

_____

3.023 enunciation _____

_____

Complete these activities (each answer, 3 points).

3.024 List the three parts of an oral report.

a. _____

b. _____

c. _____

3.025 List the five categories of an oral report's function.

a. _____

b. _____

c. _____

d. _____

e. _____

3.026 List the three kinds of dangling modifiers.

a. _____

b. _____

c. _____

Complete these statements (each answer, 3 points).

3.027 Two negative modifiers used with the verb of a sentence are called a(n) _____ .

3.028 The noun or pronoun to which a pronoun refers is called _____ .

3.029 The three moods of a verb are a. _____ , b. _____ , and c. _____ .

3.030 Words that are outdated are called _____ .

3.031 Two types of vocabulary used in casual or technical language, but rarely used in written work, are a. _____ and b. _____ .

3.032 A language that changes as it develops, adding and dropping words, is called a

_____ language.

3.033 A word that has been dropped from the language is called

_____ .

3.034 The study of language is called _____ .

Rewrite these sentences (each answer, 4 points).

3.035 Neither of us are going to the store.

_____

3.036 My mother and my sister told me that I needed a haircut, and she was right.

_____

3.037 Forgetting he was going to meet his boss, his jogging suit was the only clean clothes he had.

_____

3.038 Sit still and you ought to behave in front of company.

_____

SCORE _____   TEACHER _____ _____

initials   date

ABC **Take your spelling test of Spelling Words-3.**

Before taking the LIFEPAC Test, you may want to do one or more of these self checks.

1. _____ Read the objectives. See if you can do them.
2. _____ Restudy the material related to any objectives that you cannot do.
3. _____ Use the **SQ3R** study procedure to review the material.
4. _____ Review activities, Self Tests, and LIFEPAC vocabulary words.
5. _____ Restudy areas of weakness indicated by the last Self Test.
6. _____ Review all spelling words in this LIFEPAC.

LANGUAGE ARTS 809

LIFEPAC TEST

NAME _____

DATE _____

SCORE _____

78
___
97

LANGUAGE ARTS 809: LIFEPAC TEST

Match these items (each answer, 2 points).

1. _____ etymology
2. _____ slang
3. _____ grammar
4. _____ main body
5. _____ pentad
6. _____ enunciation
7. _____ actor-agent
8. _____ monotone
9. _____ thesis
10. _____ trade

a. helped spread and develop language
b. rules for speaking and writing
c. middle of the report
d. rarely used in writing
e. forming words carefully
f. method of organization
g. uninflected speech
h. statement of direction and purpose
i. Who?
j. the study of word origins
k. technical language

Answer true or false (each answer, 1 point).

11. _____ United States English contains many technical words.
12. _____ "Doth" is an archaic word.
13. _____ The subject of a report should be appropriate to its audience.
14. _____ An *expression* report does not require details.
15. _____ Double negatives are usually acceptable in writing.
16. _____ A *persuasion* report should be convincing.
17. _____ The English language has not changed much in the last few centuries.
18. _____ Linguistics is the study of languages.
19. _____ The main body of a report should contain supportive information.
20. _____ While speaking, you should not look directly at the audience.

Complete these statements (each answer, 3 points).

21. The three parts of an oral report are a. _____ , b. _____ , and

c. _____ .

22. The five major questions the pentad lists are a. _____ , b. _____ ,

c. _____ , d. _____ , and e. _____ .

23. Five categories explaining the function of an oral report include

a. _____ , b. _____ , c. _____ ,

d. _____ , and e. _____ .

24. Four errors to avoid include sentences with a. _____ ,

b. _____ , c. _____ , and

d. _____ .

Write an X by the correct sentence (each answer, 2 points).

25. _____ a. I can't hardly understand him.

_____ b. I can hardly understand him.

26. _____ a. Waving frantically, he flagged the train.

_____ b. Waving frantically, the train stopped.

27. _____ a. Flipping through the book, his homework paper fell out.

_____ b. Flipping through the book, he found his homework paper.

28. _____ a. To finish his meal, the steak must be eaten.

_____ b. To finish his meal, Bob must eat his steak.

29. _____ a. In eating his lunch, a bone chipped his tooth.

_____ b. In eating his lunch, Jim bit down on a bone and chipped his tooth.

30. _____ a. When eating, my baby sister always uses a bib.

_____ b. When eating, a bib is used by my baby sister.

31. _____ a. Is everybody having a good time?

_____ b. Are everybody having a good time?

32. _____ a: Either of you may bring his book.

_____ b. Either of you may bring their book.

ABC **Take your LIFEPAC Spelling Test.**